The Story of Planet Earth

This is what life in the Earth's oceans may have looked like around 400 million years ago.

The Story of Planet Earth

Abigail Wheatley

Illustrated by Sanna Mander

Designed by Samantha Barrett, Brenda Cole
and Tom Lalonde

Edited by Jane Chisholm
Consultant: Dr. Roger Trend

Internet links

There are lots of great websites you can visit for information, activities and animations about the story of Planet Earth. For links to these sites, go to the Usborne Quicklinks Website at www.usborne.com/quicklinks and enter the keywords 'Story of Planet Earth'.

Please follow the internet safety guidelines displayed on the Usborne Quicklinks website.

This photograph shows molten rock from a volcano flowing into the ocean. Processes like this have been going on for millions of years, helping to shape our planet.

Contents

This is what the Earth and the
Sun look like from space.

Planet Earth

Our planet, the Earth, has been around for
millions of years. In all that time, the only
thing about it that's stayed the same is that
it's kept on changing.
This book tells the Earth's story, from its
beginnings as a tiny blob of stardust, to the
vast and complex planet of today.
But before you set out on this astonishing
journey, it helps to know exactly where
you're starting from...

Meet our planet

Planet Earth is a huge, round, rocky ball 13,000km (8,000 miles) across. It is formed of several layers, like the layers of an onion.

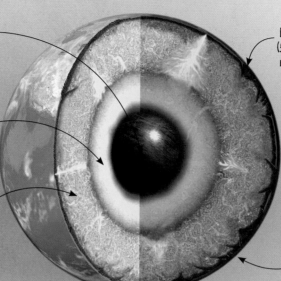

Inner core
1,300km (800 miles) across, made of super-hot metal. It is so hot it should melt, but it doesn't because it's squashed so tightly together.

Outer core
2,250km (1,400 miles) in depth, it is also super-hot metal, but it's liquid because it's less squashed.

Mantle
2,900km (1,800 mile) layer of very hot rock that's sticky in places. The heat keeps it moving around very slowly.

Crust
Between 8km and 40km (5-25 miles) in depth and made of cool, solid rock, it forms the land and the ocean floor.

Atmosphere
A layer of gases around the Earth, it is around 100km (62 miles) in height.

The moon

The moon is a rocky ball, much smaller than the Earth. It travels around the Earth in a big, squashed circle, known as an orbit.

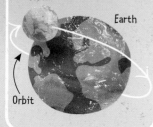

Moon

Earth

Orbit

Our local area

The Earth floats in a vast area known as space. Even the nearest thing to it, the moon, is around 385,000km (240,000 miles) away. Beyond the moon are the planets, and then the Sun, which is 150 million km (93 million miles) away.

Together, the Earth, the planets and the Sun make up the Solar System – our local patch of space. This is big, but it's actually only a tiny part of the Universe – which is the name for all of space and everything in it.

The Solar System

The Sun is a star, at the heart of the Solar System. The Earth and all the other planets travel around it in big, squashed circles, or orbits.

The Earth takes an entire year to travel along its orbit. As it travels, it also spins around. One spin takes 24 hours. It is this spinning that makes day and night: it's day in the part of the Earth that's turned towards the Sun and night in the part that's turned away.

The Earth spins and travels at an angle, so different parts of it are tilted towards or away from the Sun at different times of year. This makes some parts of the Earth's surface hotter and some parts colder. That's what creates the seasons.

Leaning planet

The Earth spins, a little like a bead on a wire. Where the wire would be is an imaginary line known as the axis. This is tilted at an angle to the Earth's orbit around the Sun.

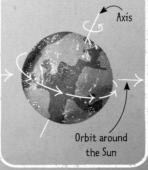

Axis

Orbit around the Sun

The Sun

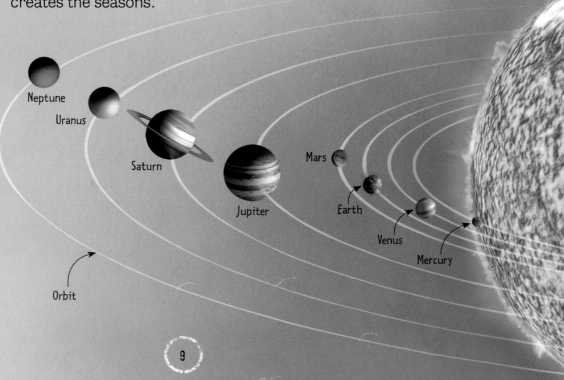

Neptune

Uranus

Saturn

Jupiter

Mars

Earth

Venus

Mercury

Orbit

This image of the Earth's surface shows blue oceans, brown land and swirling white clouds.

This diagram shows what happens when the Sun, heating up the land and sea at different rates, makes wind.

On the surface

Surprisingly, almost three-quarters of the Earth is covered by water. The oceans can be vast, deep and icy, or small, shallow, warm and tropical. The rest of the Earth's surface is land – from tiny islands to vast continents, and from hot deserts to snowy mountains.

Making the weather

This contrast between the land and the oceans is what powers the weather. When the Sun shines, the land heats up more quickly than the sea. This temperature difference makes the air move, creating wind, which carries clouds, rain and snow around the world.

Wind

The air over the land is warm, so it rises.

Air rushes across to fill the gaps made by falling and rising air.

The moving air is wind.

Wind

The air over the sea is cool, so it sinks.

The land heats up fast, becoming warm.

The sea heats up slowly, staying cool.

Where there's life

The most extraordinary thing about our planet's surface is that it is home to millions of living things. There are microscopic living cells; plants ranging from slimy pondweeds to vast trees; bugs that crawl, swim and fly; and animals from earthworms, jellyfish, sharks, eagles and lizards to people, who are animals too.

Necessities of life

All living things depend on water and sunlight – and other living things. For example, animals need water to drink, and they need plants (and sometimes other animals) to eat. Plants need water and sunlight too, and some rely on animals to carry their seeds to new places so new plants can grow. So, living things across the planet all need each other to survive.

Oasis in space

The Earth is the only planet where we can be certain living things exist. Not even a single live cell has been found anywhere else in the entire Universe. Ever. That makes our planet pretty amazingly special.

So how did it get to be like that? To find out, you have to go back a really long way, to a time before the planet was even there at all...

Biosphere

The zone where life exists is known as the *biosphere*. In height it reaches from the ocean depths to high in the sky. In breadth it stretches around the entire planet.

This image shows where there are most living things in the biosphere. On land the densest areas of life are green, fading to yellow where there's less life. In the oceans, paler blue areas have most life, dark blue and purple areas have less.

Why on Earth?

It is because of the Earth's water that things can live here. It's lucky the Earth is just where it is. If it was closer to the Sun, the water would dry up. If it was further away, the water would freeze. Either way, nothing could live here.

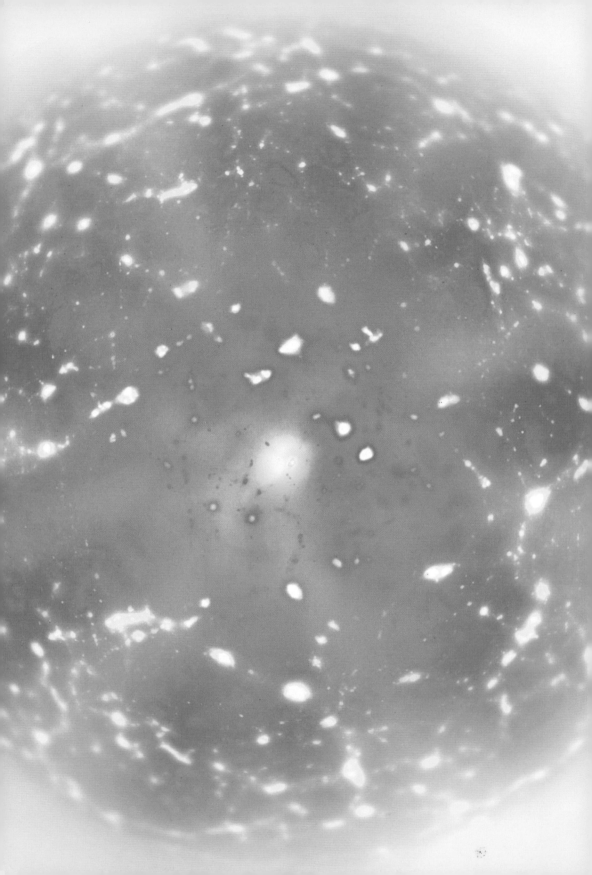

Big Bang

It all started just over thirteen billion years
ago. There were no planets, no stars – not
even any time or space existed yet. But there
was one astonishingly tiny point, packed full
of all the stuff in the Universe.
That sounds incredible, and it was – much
too incredible to last. The tiny point suddenly
blasted apart in the biggest explosion there
has ever been. We call it the Big Bang.
The Universe had begun.

This picture may help you to imagine the Big
Bang. But if you'd been there you wouldn't
actually have seen or heard anything –
because sound and light didn't exist yet.

After the Big Bang

A few seconds after...

The Universe grew at an
unbelievable speed and heated up
to mind-blowing temperatures.

Masses of incredibly tiny
particles of super-heated stuff
whizzed out in all directions.

A few minutes after...

The Universe began to cool down
a little. It also slowed down bit
by bit – it was still growing, but
not quite so quickly.

Nothing else happened for a
very, very long time.

400,000 years after...

Some of the particles cooled
down enough to clump together,
forming atoms – slightly bigger
(but still very, very tiny) particles.

All these early atoms were very
light gas atoms. They hung in vast
gas clouds in space.

Life cycle of a star

A nuclear reaction inside a star may go on for millions of years, but eventually it burns out. When this happens, some stars shrink, but others grow, and some of these ones explode.

For the first 90% of a star's life it burns steadily.

Then, some stars grow much bigger, and become cooler.

Finally, some of them blow up in a vast explosion known as a supernova.

200 million years after...

Some parts of the gas clouds collapsed in on themselves. This started nuclear reactions that burned the gas, creating giant gas fireballs. These were the first stars.

The nuclear reactions inside some of the stars rearranged the gas atoms, making new, heavier atoms.

9 billion years after...

At the end of their lives, some stars exploded, scattering heavy atoms into space as stardust.

In a cloud of stardust and gas, a new star formed. It was our Sun.

From the Sun to the Earth

When the Sun formed around 4.7 billion years ago, in some ways it was like millions of other stars. But, in other ways, it was rather different.

When its nuclear reaction started up, it trapped a massive, super-hot, doughnut-shaped cloud of gas and stardust that swirled and spun around it. If this hadn't happened, our planet would never have existed

This is how our Sun may have looked around 4.7 billion years ago, when it was first formed.

Doughnut spotting

The Sun isn't the only star to have trapped a doughnut-shaped dusty gas cloud. Using very powerful telescopes that float in space, scientists today can see similar clouds around other stars.

Clumping together

As the hot gas and dust grains swept around the Sun in the dusty cloud, they crashed and smashed into each other. Each time they crashed, they clumped together into larger and larger blobs.

Bigger and bigger

After around 20 million years, the biggest blobs had grown to the size of planets. Amazingly, that's exactly what they were: the planets of the Solar System, circling around the Sun. And one of them – a medium-sized, hard one, quite close to the Sun – was the Earth.

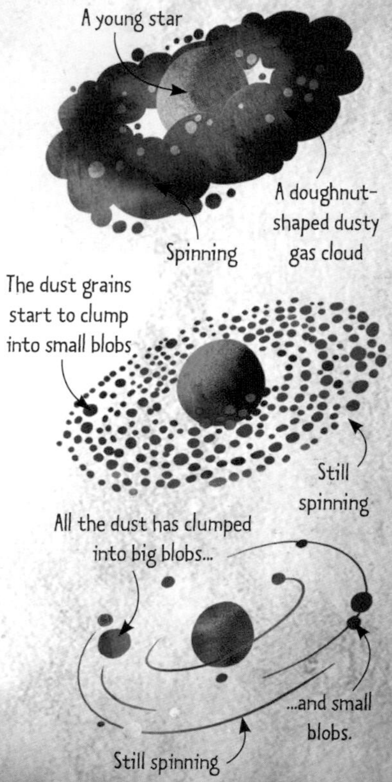

Early Earth

So, the Earth was formed from rocky blobs of stardust that contained different types of atoms thrown out by ancient stars. The heaviest atoms – metals such as iron – had sunk deep inside, so the Earth had a massive ball of iron at its heart. Around the iron core was a layer of super-hot melted rock, which was constantly pounded by chunks of rock left over from the dusty cloud.

This picture shows the Earth around 4.5 billion years ago, being pounded by rocky lumps of stardust.

How planets form

A young star

A doughnut-shaped dusty gas cloud

Spinning

The dust grains start to clump into small blobs

Still spinning

All the dust has clumped into big blobs...

...and small blobs.

Still spinning

The crash and after

① Theia is on a collision course with the Earth.

Earth

Theia

② Theia crashes into the Earth at great speed.

Theia breaks up.

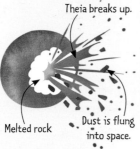

Melted rock

Dust is flung into space.

③ Melted rock flows over the entire planet.

Dust from Theia circles around the Earth.

The dust clumps into blobs.

④ The Earth cools. The dust forms the moon.

Earth

Moon

The Big Whack

Small rocks crashing into the Earth didn't make much impact. But imagine it happening with a rock the size of a small planet. A collision that massive would change the planet forever.

According to experts, this is just what happened soon after the Earth formed. They call it the Big Whack.

Theia

The rock that's supposed to have hit the Earth was Theia: a planet-like mass, one-third the size of the early Earth. When Theia hit the Earth, it punched a vast hole. The impact created colossal amounts of heat, melting the Earth's rocks. Seas of molten rock poured over the surface of the planet, eventually filling in the hole that Theia had created.

The aftermath

Experts think Theia was smashed to pieces by the impact. Some pieces probably melted and sank into the melted rocks of the Earth. Other pieces, along with some of the Earth's rocks, were crushed to dust, which circled around the planet. Over hundreds of years, this dust clumped into bigger and bigger blobs, until it formed the moon.

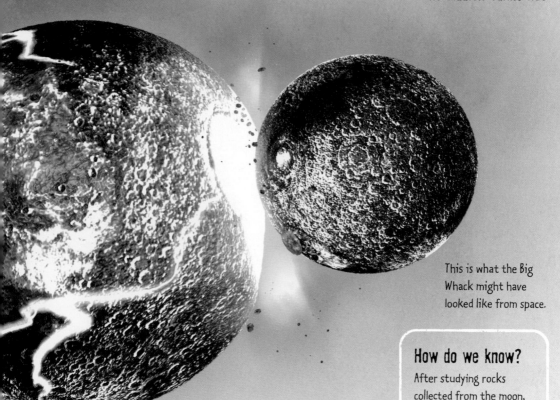

This is what the Big Whack might have looked like from space.

How do we know?

After studying rocks collected from the moon, scientists found out that they might have been formed by a giant collision. That's how they came up with the Big Whack theory.

Little whacks

After the Big Whack, there were no more massive rocky lumps circling around in the Solar System. So the Big Whack couldn't happen again.

But there were still plenty of small rocky lumps, which kept on crashing into the Earth, and into the moon, too. That's why, even today, the moon is covered in huge holes, known as craters. Craters formed on the Earth too. But, since then, so much has happened to the Earth's surface that they've disappeared.

This is how the Earth may have looked 4,000 million years ago. The temperature on the surface was around 15 times hotter than it is now, and the gases in the atmosphere made the sky look orange.

Greenhouse effect

This is how gases in the Earth's atmosphere trap the Sun's heat. It's known as the *greenhouse effect*. It started millions of years ago, and is still going on today.

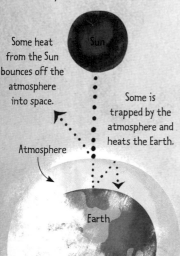

Some heat from the Sun bounces off the atmosphere into space.

Sun

Some is trapped by the atmosphere and heats the Earth.

Atmosphere

Earth

Molten planet

After the Big Whack, the Earth began to cool down slightly. But, even so, for the next few million years it was still incredibly hot. Fiery liquid rock flowed out into great lakes and spouted up in vast volcanoes.

There was water too, but it was incredibly hot and created scalding pools and clouds of steam. They dissolved the Earth's rocks, releasing clouds of gas.

Hot water

The steam and gas built up into a layer known as the atmosphere. This trapped the planet's heat and kept it scaldingly hot for millions of years.

Eventually, around 4 billion years ago, rocks stopped crashing into the Earth and the planet cooled down. The steam in the atmosphere turned to water, which fell as the first rain.

Land and sea

The rain helped the rocks to cool and harden into a lumpy surface. Water ran down to collect in the hollows, forming the first oceans. The parts that stuck up out of the water formed the first land.

Beneath the surface, the liquid rock also cooled a little, forming a layer that flowed stickily around. Its movements made the rock above it crack into around twenty vast sections, or plates. And, very slowly, these began to move.

Crunching and bunching

Over millions of years, as the plates moved, they collided or ripped apart. Gradually, these movements would form huge volcanoes and mountain chains, shaping the planet's surface.

Meanwhile, as these vast processes were just starting, tiny – but incredibly important – changes were also happening...

Moving plates

Even today, the Earth's surface is made up of plates, and they're still moving and changing shape – but so slowly you'd never even notice it...

A plate

Another plate

This diagram shows what can happen when the plates of the Earth's surface collide.

Sometimes, two plates crash right into each other. The rock piles up into a mountain range.

Sometimes, one plate dives under the edge of another plate. The rock bulges up into islands and volcanoes.

First life

Around 3.7 billion years ago, the first ever
living thing came into being. It was a tiny,
simple soft blob or cell, filled with a watery
mixture of dissolved chemicals. But somehow
– no one knows how – it came to life.
It began to take in chemicals from the
world around it and broke them down into
food. Even more astonishingly, it started
to create lots more tiny, living cells just like
itself. Life on Earth had begun.

This photograph shows a naturally hot
pool in Wyoming, USA. The reddish stains
in the water are very simple living cells.
Scientists think the first living things
may have started in places like this.

Life – the theories

In warm pools full of dissolved chemicals, lightning or sunlight could have started chemical reactions that created life.

Maybe life started because of chemical reactions near deep sea vents, where heat and chemicals welled up from under the Earth's crust.

Or it's possible that living cells, or the chemicals needed to make them, fell to Earth from space, on a lump of space rock.

Small beginnings

There are several theories about how life began. But life as we know it couldn't have started without water and carbon. It was water, full of dissolved chemicals, that allowed living cells to break things down into food. And it was carbon that held each cell together. Even today, all living things need carbon and water.

There was plenty of both water and carbon on the early Earth. Carbon was one of the atoms created inside stars, and it was mixed into many of the Earth's rocks and gases. And, of course, the oceans were full of water.

Food and water

All early cells lived in water. They took in gases and chemicals from the water around them for food and energy. And, surprisingly, they thrived in places where the water was full of strong chemicals, very salty and, often, extremely hot.

Getting together

Many early cells were still just tiny, soft blobs. Others joined together in long chains, or wide, mat- or cushion-like layers, glued together by grains of mud or sand. They may have looked like a little like stony lumps, but in fact they were made of living things.

Going pink

Soon, some cells started to use sunlight to break down water and carbon dioxide gas (CO_2) into food and oxygen gas. This is known as photosynthesis. It's what plants do today.

These cells needed the food so they could grow and copy themselves, but they didn't need the oxygen. They just puffed this out. Gradually, as more and more cells grew, oxygen began to build up in the water and the atmosphere. Very slowly, the oxygen began to turn the sky and seas from browny orange to purply pink.

The Earth may have looked like this around 3,000 million years ago. The lumps at the bottom of the picture are formed of layers of cells, held together by mud.

Making new cells

Each early living cell contained a cluster of chemicals that told it how to copy itself.

First, the chemical instructions copied themselves, and told the cell to start splitting.

When the splitting finished, there were two new cells, both the same as the first cell.

These photosynthesizing cells are similar to ones that lived 3,000 million years ago. The one on the right is copying itself by dividing into two.

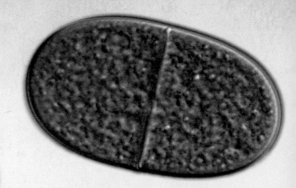

Growing and changing

Life could have stayed like this pretty much forever. Except that some cells gradually started to change. This often happened because a cell or its instructions were damaged.

Evolution

Small, random changes in living things don't sound very important. But masses of tiny changes, over millions of years, can add up to huge changes.

It was through many tiny changes that cells gradually transformed into simple plants and animals, and then into the huge variety of living things alive today. This process is known as *evolution*.

Being different

When a damaged cell split, the new cells it made were slightly different. These differences could be good or bad. Sometimes they meant the cell couldn't survive. But sometimes they helped it to survive better. In this way, new types of cells developed, living alongside the old types.

Moving in together

Cells changed in other ways, too. Some started eating each other. Things didn't always end badly for the cell that was eaten. Some carried on living inside the cells that had eaten them. Both divided at the same time, producing new cells that already had other cells living inside them.

The big cell on the right has just eaten some small cells – you can still see them inside it. They are similar to the small cells below.

Accidents happen

Chance also played a big part in which types of cells survived. For example, especially hot – or cold – weather might kill off one type of cell, while another type flourished.

Variety of life

Over time, even though some types of cells died out, the number of different types increased, and many of them were becoming more and more complex. In fact, before very long there were so many cells that they actually began to change the world around them.

Changing the planet

By 850 million years ago, oxygen puffed out by photosynthesizing cells had built up in the atmosphere and water. This turned the sea and sky clear and blue, but it also poisoned some cells, killing them off forever. But another lethal change was about to take place.

Natural selection

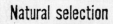

Evolution produces some creatures that are better than others at surviving. So, a cell that's good at eating will survive and make lots of copies of itself. Cells that aren't so good may die out.

This idea, known as *natural selection*, is part of evolution. One of the first people to think of it was British naturalist Charles Darwin, born in 1809.

On reflection

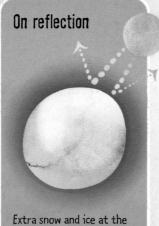

Extra snow and ice at the time of Snowball Earth made it extra difficult for the planet to keep warm. That's because white things reflect heat away, so more of the Sun's heat bounced back into space.

Some living cells are at home in freezing ice and snow. This photograph shows red and green photosynthesizing cells in Antarctica, the coldest part of the world today. Similar cells may have survived at the time of Snowball Earth.

Snowball Earth

Around 850 million years ago, the amount of carbon dioxide gas (CO_2) in the atmosphere suddenly dropped dramatically.

No one knows just why this happened. But CO_2 traps some of the Sun's heat in the atmosphere, warming the Earth. So a sudden drop in CO_2 meant that more of the Sun's heat bounced off the Earth, back into space.

The surface of the planet started to freeze. It kept on freezing for millions of years. This icy period is sometimes known as Snowball Earth.

Dying out

The sudden drop in temperature was too much for most types of living cells. Many died out, never to return.

It could have been the end of life on Earth. But, amazingly, some cells managed to cling on to life through 200 million years of bitter cold.

Mass extinction

Snowball Earth wasn't the last time life on Earth would almost be wiped out. In fact, over the rest of the Earth's history, dramatic changes in temperature would happen every few million years, killing off many living things. These are known as *mass extinction events*. But, each time, enough living things survived to begin life again once the disaster was over.

During Snowball Earth, the planet may have looked like this. Vast areas were covered in snow and ice, but there was some clear land and sea.

The big melt

This was exactly what happened after Snowball Earth. Eventually, after 200 million years of bitter cold, Snowball Earth came to an end. Somehow, CO_2 gradually built up in the atmosphere again, and the snow and ice melted.

Volcano power

Scientists think Snowball Earth ended thanks to volcanoes pumping CO_2 into the atmosphere. This would have trapped more of the Sun's heat again, keeping the Earth warm.

Growing again

The warmer temperatures made things much easier for the few living cells that had survived. They were free to multiply, grow and change. By around 500 million years ago, the Earth's seas were full of a fascinating array not just of cells, but of much more complex things.

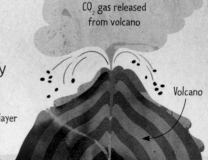

CO_2 gas released from volcano

Volcano

Ice layer

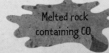

Melted rock containing CO_2

This is how parts of the oceans may have looked 500 million years ago.

Life goes big

By around 530 million years ago, the warm, shallow seas of planet Earth teemed with a huge variety of life. There were still some tiny single-celled creatures, and some simple creatures made from little bundles of cells. But, by now, more complex creatures had evolved too.

Complex creatures

Their bodies were built from hundreds or even thousands of cells, all working together. Some of them were like today's corals and sponges. They were fixed to the sea floor and caught passing food in their tentacles.

Eating each other

There were also small, worm-like creatures that ate the spongy things. Fiercer, larger animals ate the worms. Some meat-eating animals swam or floated around searching for smaller creatures to eat, while others crept along or burrowed into the sea bed.

Complex creatures

Some of these creatures looked unlike anything living now, but many of them were distant ancestors of animals that are still around today. So, life as we know it had begun. But the next big change was only just around the corner.

Muddy fossils

Many fossils of creatures from this period were found in 1909 by American fossil expert Charles Walcott, in rocks in Canada. The ancient creatures became fossils after underwater mud banks collapsed, burying them.

This small, hard-shelled creature is called a *trilobite*. Around 500 million years ago, many of these scuttled along the sea bed in search of food.

Here are some of the creatures that lived in the
crowded oceans around 500 million years ago.
The large squid-like animal, a *nautiloid*, is about
to pounce on a trilobite. There are also some
shells similar to today's mussels.

Leaving the seas

The Earth's oceans may have been
teeming with life, but they were also
difficult and dangerous places, crowded
with fierce creatures all in search of food.
It wasn't long before some creatures
struggled out onto the bare and desolate
land, just to try to survive.

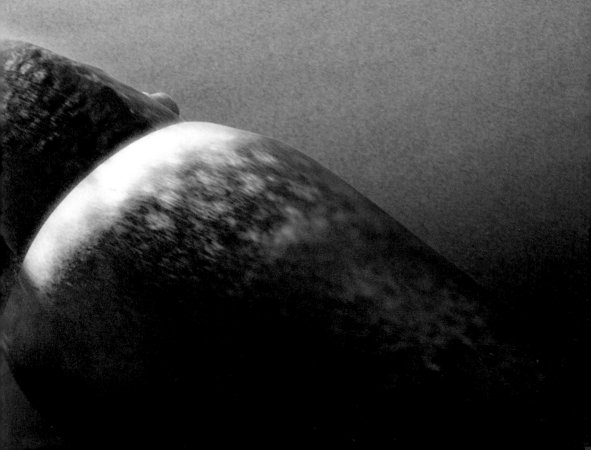

Land plants

This is *Aglaophyton*, an early land plant. Instead of roots, it had thin, thread-like structures that drew up water from the surface of the ground.

The first steps

Only some types of creatures could survive on land, even for a short time. Living things had evolved in water, and needed it to breathe, move and reproduce.

Many plants and animals were soft and floppy. Out in the air, their bodies would have collapsed in a mushy heap. But there were others that were much better suited to living on dry land.

Plants make the move

The first plants to move to land had a tough outer covering that kept in moisture and helped them to stand upright. But, even so, they could only survive in damp places, such as the edges of seas, rivers or lakes.

This is how early land plants may have looked around 400 million years ago, growing on the damp margins of a lake.

The first land animals

The first land animals probably looked something like trilobites. They had hard coverings known as *exoskeletons*. In water, these had protected the animals from being eaten, but on land, they supported their bodies and prevented them from drying out.

Fossil tracks

Experts have found fossilized tracks, made by creatures' feet sinking into damp mud. That's how we know that some animals were scuttling onto land at this time.

Getting used to life on land

Like plants, the first land animals stayed close to water, probably just scuttling onto land for part of the time. But, over millions of years, plants and animals became suited to life on land, and many shapes and sizes developed.

As early plants adapted to land, they grew bigger. These plants, *Calamites*, grew to 3.5m (11ft) tall.

The first soil

Early plants died and rotted into sand or mud, making a shallow layer of soil.

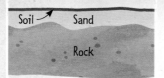

Soil →   Sand

Rock

The soil helped more plants to grow. They rotted, making more soil.

Gradually, the soil became deep enough for plants with longer roots.

Life on land

By 400 million years ago, land plants had developed stiffer, more waterproof coverings, and roots to suck water from under the ground. This helped to create soil – a moist, rich layer on top of the ground, ideal for plants to grow in.

Plants could now move away from water and grow deeper roots. By 380 million years ago, the first trees had developed.

Creepy-crawlies

Land animals were changing, too. By now, hard-shelled millipedes and centipedes, cockroaches, scorpions, wingless insects and spider-like creatures were creeping around.

Soil problem

Soil was great for plants, and land animals could also burrow into it, for shelter. But when it rained, chemicals from the soil washed into lakes and rivers, making it hard for some creatures that lived there to breathe.

Fish out of water

Soon, some fish with backbones and fins were moving to land. They gulped air at the water's surface, and used their bony fins to push themselves around the beds of lakes and rivers.

Later, some developed muscly legs that could walk underwater, and lungs that could breathe air properly. Gradually, they started spending more time out of water and on land. Their bones helped them to stand up.

Living fossils

Coelacanths are fish with backbones and bony fins. They developed around 400 million years ago, and were closely related to the first types of fish with lungs and legs. But the most amazing thing about Coelacanths is that they are still around today.

This is *Ichthyostega*, one of the first creatures with lungs and a backbone to live partly on land. In front of it you can see a millipede and two cockroaches.

Carbon sponges

At this time there were lush forests that soaked up CO_2 from the air. When the plants died, many were buried under mud. This trapped their carbon underground. Over millions of years, the plants hardened into fossils, made of a carbon-rich rock named coal.

Coal

Surviving fires

Some plants may have adapted to cope with the frequent wild fires that swept forests 360 million years ago.

For example, it's possible that fire made *Lepidodendron* (a giant, tree-sized moss) release some of its seeds, and made the seeds sprout faster, so new plants grew.

The first forests

By 360 million years ago, lush forests covered much of the land. Tall trees towered over dense undergrowth of huge vines, ferns and mosses.

All these plants used sunlight to break water and CO_2 into food, locking away carbon in their stems, wood and leaves, and giving off oxygen. There were so many plants that this changed the planet's atmosphere: there was more oxygen in the air than ever before or since.

Wild fires

The increase in oxygen had several effects. Oxygen helps things to burn. So, when lightning struck a tree during a storm, it started to blaze very easily. There were a great many forest fires, though the plants and animals seem to have survived them pretty well.

Land giants

The high level of oxygen also made it very easy for land animals to breathe, and many of them began to grow to vast sizes. Millipedes 180cm (6ft) long trundled through the undergrowth and 60cm (2ft) scorpions lurked under fallen trunks. By now, some insects could fly. Vast dragonflies flitted in and out of the forest glades.

In and out of water

There were now many types of fishy creatures with legs and lungs. Some lived on land most of the time, but returned to water to keep their skin moist, and to lay their soft eggs. These types of creatures are known as *amphibians*.

Land only

But some amphibians adapted to land so well that they could live completely away from the water. They became the first *reptiles*.

This is how a forest might have looked around 300 million years ago. The huge dragonfly, *Meganeura*, had a 75cm (2.5ft) wingspan.

Jelly eggs

This is *Eryops*, a type of early amphibian. It probably laid its soft, jelly-like eggs in water, attached to water plants.

Leathery eggs

Early reptiles probably laid their eggs in sandy burrows on land. Each egg contained liquids to protect and feed the baby developing inside its leathery shell.

The first reptiles

Reptiles evolved from amphibians, but the difference was that they had scaly skin that kept in moisture. Even their eggs had leathery shells that stopped them from drying out.

Reptiles were cold-blooded, too. This meant they relied on the Sun to warm their bodies. Each morning, they lay in the sunshine until their bodies heated up. Then, they could move around and look for food. At night, when they were cold, they needed to rest.

Dimetrodon was a large, sail-backed, meat-eating reptile that lived around 250 million years ago. Some Dimetrodons grew as long as 4m (13ft). They were among the largest land animals of their time.

Spreading out

Soon, all kinds of different reptiles had developed and spread across the land. Many were plant-eaters, but others ate other reptiles, or different animals. Some developed sail-like structures on their backs, to help them to catch the Sun's warmth. And some even had hair, to help keep them warm.

Here are some theories about what might have caused a mass extinction event 250 million years ago.

A huge lump of space rock – or asteroid – crashing into the Earth could have triggered a vast explosion, set off volcanoes and released deadly gases.

The Great Dying

Then, around 250 million years ago, the Earth was hit by the worst mass extinction there has ever been. No one knows exactly what caused it. Perhaps a massive space rock crashed into the Earth, or vast amounts of molten rock erupted from under the Earth's crust. Or maybe there was a huge release of methane, a deadly gas. It's even possible all three happened at once. But whatever it was, it was so catastrophic that it's sometimes known as the Great Dying.

Erupting volcanoes could have covered land in molten rock and thrown dust into the air, blocking out light and poisoning the air and water.

Dying out

Out of every 100 different types of living things on Earth, 83 died out entirely. But even with such an appalling death toll, life went on. Reptiles were some of the first of the survivors to bounce back in a big way. They were about to become *dinosaurs*.

Methane, a deadly gas released from under the oceans, could have poisoned living creatures and caused the planet to heat up, killing yet more creatures.

Dinosaurs like these lived around 150 million years ago. They belonged to a group of big, heavy dinosaurs, known as *sauropods*.

Age of dinosaurs

The first dinosaurs appeared around 230 million years ago. For the next 165 million years, dinosaurs – and other reptiles – dominated the entire planet, developing an amazing variety of different shapes, sizes and lifestyles.

Dinosaurs

Between 230 and 65 million years ago, thousands of types of dinosaurs appeared. Some were as small as chickens, while others towered over the tallest trees. There were even some that grew feathery wings and flew or glided from tree to tree. This dinosaur timeline shows just a few different varieties.

Eoraptor was the size of a large dog.

230 million years ago
The first dinosaurs were called *theropods*. They ran on their back legs, seizing prey with their sharp claws.

This is *Hylaeosaurus*. Its plates helped to protect it from other dinosaurs.

Stegosaurus probably used its plates for soaking up warmth from the Sun.

135 million years ago
There were also *ankylosaurs*. They were plant eaters that were completely covered in bony plates.

140 million years ago
By now, *stegosaurs* had evolved. They had rows of plates along their backs.

112 million years ago
Plant-eaters needed protection because some theropods had grown much bigger.

This hadrosaur, called *Maiasaura*, laid its eggs in nests made from earth.

Giganotosaurus was a fierce, fast theropod.

80 million years ago
Hadrosaurs were agile plant-eaters with hard, bird-like beaks and lots of small teeth for grinding up leaves.

This is *Liliensternus*. It probably ate smaller dinosaurs.

Shunosaurus had a spiky knob on its tail for fighting enemies.

200 million years ago

Some theropods began to get bigger. Some also had hollow bones, which meant they could run faster, too.

170 million years ago

By now, *sauropods* had appeared. They were slow plant-eaters, with long necks and big bodies.

Archaeopteryx probably flew or glided from tree to tree.

Supersaurus was one of the largest dinosaurs ever. It grew to around 33m (108ft) long.

150 million years ago

Some theropods had developed wings and feathers.

145 million years ago

Sauropods were getting very big indeed.

Triceratops had three sharp horns to scare away predators.

Tyrannosaurus rex was by far the largest meat-eater of its time.

67 million years ago

By now the *ceratopsians* had evolved. They had bony frills and horns on their heads.

65 million years ago

And the theropods were scarier than ever before...

Big country

At this time, most of the Earth's land was joined together in one huge mass, known as *Pangaea*. It was surrounded by a vast sea, known as *Panthalassa*. Pangaea later split up to create today's continents.

This is a *plesiosaur*. It breathed air, but spent almost all its life underwater.

Not-dinosaurs

Dinosaurs all belonged to one large group of reptiles. But there were also other groups of reptiles that weren't dinosaurs, but lived alongside them.

Sea reptiles

Some non-dinosaur reptiles had made the move into the oceans. The earliest ones simply used their legs to paddle around in the water for part of the time.

But, over millions of years, some developed smoother bodies and flippers for swimming, and spent their lives beneath the waves. They only came to the surface to take gulps of air. Some were similar to crocodiles and turtles, but others were sleek, with long necks and sharp teeth for snapping up fish.

High fliers

On land, many different types of non-dinosaur reptiles flourished. Some evolved leathery wings and took to the air, flying low over lakes and oceans to scoop up fish and other small creatures. Others were similar to today's snakes and lizards.

Fast and furry

Some land reptiles even grew fur. Over time, they developed the ability to make heat inside their bodies, rather than needing the Sun's warmth. This meant they could come out and look for food at night, and stay out of the way of fierce reptiles in the day. Eventually, they became the first *mammals*.

This is a type of *pterosaur*, or winged reptile. It's known as *Pteronodon*, and was one of the larger flying reptiles, with a wingspan of over 6m (20ft).

Milk makers

As well as being furry and being able to heat themselves, mammals also shared another feature. Mammal mothers fed their babies on milk made inside their bodies.

It's possible a vast asteroid like this one crashed into the Earth around 65 million years ago, with devastating effects.

Smashing idea

Two American scientists, father and son Walter and Luis Alvarez, came up with the idea that an asteroid wiped out the dinosaurs. They found evidence for a huge impact in rocks formed at the time the dinosaurs died out.

End of the dinosaurs

Suddenly, around 65 million years ago, almost all the dinosaurs – and many other types of plants and animals – died out. The cause may have been a vast asteroid crashing into Earth.

Impact event

This would have caused *tsunamis* (giant waves), earthquakes and volcanic eruptions. Dust would have been thrown up into the air, blocking out light and poisoning air and water. CO_2 released by volcanoes would have warmed up the planet dramatically.

More mass extinction

Whether or not an asteroid was to blame, there was certainly a world-wide disaster. Plants on land and in the sea couldn't get enough sunlight to make food, so they all died. That meant plant-eaters couldn't survive. So, the meat-eaters that ate the plant-eaters died out too.

All the flying reptiles, almost all the dinosaurs and almost all the water-dwelling reptiles (and many other sea-creatures) became extinct.

The survivors

Only a few small, tough animals, including some insects, birds, reptiles, amphibians and mammals, survived the disaster. They probably burrowed into the ground or the sea floor to find shelter and ate what they could, including the decaying remains of dead plants and animals.

Life goes on

The survivors couldn't have kept going if plants had become extinct. But, before they died, some plants produced seeds that lay safely in the ground. As things calmed down, the seeds sprouted, plants returned and the survivors could begin to live normal lives again.

Living dinosaurs?

Maybe not all dinosaurs died out 65 million years ago. Recently, scientists have decided that today's birds are a type of dinosaur, as they developed directly from dinosaurs. So, in a way, some dinosaurs are still alive.

Fossil ferns

Ferns were some of the first plants to recover. Experts know this because they have found fern seeds (known as *spores*) in rocks formed just after the mass extinction.

Long legs

Claw

Bat flaps

Fossils of early bats show that they had long back legs, and claws on each finger. They probably glided along between each flap of their wings.

The rise of the mammals

Out of all the survivors, it was the mammals that really took off. Over the next few million years, thousands of different types developed and many of them took the places of the dinosaurs that had died out.

So, as well as small, scurrying night mammals, there were now huge, slow, plant-eating mammals. These were hunted by faster, fiercer, meat-eating ones. Some mammals moved to the seas, becoming the first whales and dolphins, while other mammals – the bats – took to the skies on leathery wings.

This huge early plant-eating mammal is known as *Megacerops*. An adult stood around 2.5m (8.2ft) tall – one and a half times the size of a modern rhino.

Prime position

Mammals were now the fastest, strongest and most intelligent creatures around. But there was one group that was even more brainy than the others – the *primates*.

Some early primates may have looked something like this. They probably ate fruit and leaves and spent much of their lives in the trees.

Agile and brainy

The first primates were small, squirrel-like mammals that lived in trees. They developed sensitive fingers and toes, so they could move along branches easily. They also had forward-facing eyes and big brains that helped them to judge distances well when jumping and climbing.

Over the next few million years, creatures like these developed in ways that opened up an entirely new chapter in the story of Planet Earth.

Ida's tale

In 1983 a very complete fossil of an early primate, nicknamed Ida, was discovered near Messel in Germany. The fossil formed 47 million years ago when Ida breathed in poisonous gas bubbling up from a lake. She fell into the water and was quickly buried in mud at the bottom.

Chimpanzees are primates. They're related to the earliest apes, and also to modern humans. Like us, they enjoy each other's company, communicate with one another other and use tools.

Primate power

Around 30 million years ago, some primates
with especially big brains developed into
monkeys and apes. They lived in trees
but also spent time on the ground, mostly
walking around on all fours. Gradually, some
began to walk upright for more and more of
the time. By 5 million years ago, they had
become the first ever people. And, over
the next 5 million years, their descendants
would take over the entire planet.

Stone bones

Only a few remains of the first people have survived, as fossilized bones. This is all that remains of the skeleton of an early upright primate who lived around 3.2 million years ago in what is now Ethiopia, in East Africa. She is nicknamed Lucy.

The first people

It's thought early upright primates – the first people – lived in small groups on the wide, grassy plains of East Africa. Walking upright gave them certain advantages.

Because they could see over the top of the grass, they could keep a good look out for fierce animals creeping up on them. This meant they could keep themselves and their families safe, and had a better chance of surviving.

This is what Lucy may have looked like when she was alive. She probably stood around 1.1m (3ft 7in) tall. She is shown here with a baby and another member of her family.

Hunting and gathering

Upright primates were also more efficient at finding food. Their extra height from the ground meant they could see the animals they hunted – and the plants they gathered – from a greater distance. So, they were able to plan their food collecting trips more efficiently.

Hands for holding

Because they walked upright, the first people also had their hands free. They used them to carry simple tools, such as sharp rocks or sticks, to crack open nuts or cut animal skin. Over time, they made more sophisticated tools. By 2.5 million years ago, some were sharpening stones and using them to cut up meat.

Toolmakers

Tools made it much easier for the first people to catch more animals and eat more meat. A meaty diet gave them more energy, so they probably had healthier, longer lives.

But it was good for them as a group, too. Over millions of years, their brains gradually grew bigger and more intelligent, making them even better at cooperating, hunting and surviving. Their numbers kept growing and they spread out across different parts of Africa.

Fossil footprints

By studying fossilized footprints, experts have found out how early people walked. The prints were made 3.5 million years ago at Laetoli in Tanzania, Africa, when a group of early people walked in a layer of ash from a nearby volcano.

Stone tools

Early stone tools were made by hitting one pebble carefully with another, to break off chips. The sharp edges left on the pebble, and the chips too, could be used for cutting.

Old flame
The first early people to use fire didn't know how to make it. They may have waited for lightning to strike a tree and collected burning branches.

Big and hairy
Animals as well as people had to adapt to the cold of the last Ice Age. Animals such as mammoths grew thick, shaggy hair up to 1m (3ft) long. Early people hunted mammoths for their meat, and used their bones and skins to build shelters.

New skills

By around 2 million years ago, early people had developed new, more sophisticated skills. They made complex wood and stone tools for hunting and cutting up meat. They also used fire to cook and keep warm – which meant they could live in colder climates and travel out of Africa, all across Asia and Europe.

Growing apart

As people spread over the world, they developed in different ways. Some were strong and hairy with especially big brains. Others were slimmer and less hairy. These different types of early people may have met and lived side by side.

But, around 200,000 years ago, modern people – or humans – developed. Not long after this, all the other types of early people died out. No one is quite sure why, but it may have been to do with changes in the climate.

The last Ice Age

At this time, temperatures across the world dropped and vast ice sheets covered the land. This is often known as the last Ice Age. It's possible some types of early people couldn't survive in this new, colder world.

Keeping warm

But humans had the survival skills to cope. As well as being able to make fire, they sewed warm clothes and built shelters from branches, animal bones and skins.

They also crafted canoes to travel across water and wove baskets for carrying their belongings. This meant they could travel more easily to the places where there was most food.

Bony homes

Around 15,000 years ago, people were using mammoth bones and skins to build shelters like this one.

Creative types

Despite their harsh living conditions, Ice Age humans somehow found the time and energy to make art. They carved and painted delicate animal shapes onto rocks, animal bones and deer antlers. Some of their art has survived, and it's still breathtaking even today.

Ice Age people painted these pictures of deer, wild cattle and horses onto the walls of caves at Lascaux, France, around 19,000 years ago. To make the paints, they ground up rocks and mixed them with animal fat or plant sap.

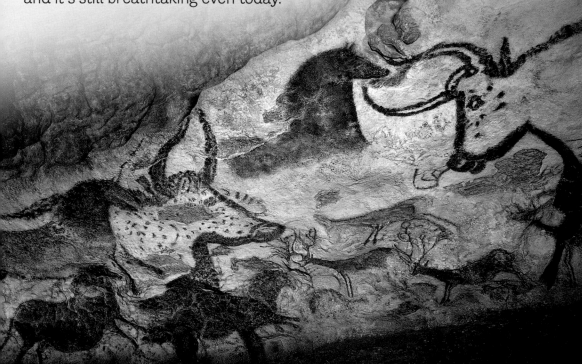

Settling down

Around 12,000 years ago, the Earth's climate gradually warmed again and plants and animals flourished. People were able to find enough food in one place, so they settled down, building permanent huts and living in them all year round.

Soon, people discovered they could tame animals, keeping them to use their milk, meat and skin. They did the same with plants, collecting wild seeds and planting them so they could harvest them easily. Farming had arrived.

Tame wolves

Before people started taming animals for farming, they brought baby wolves to live with them, to help them hunt wild animals. These gradually developed into the first dogs.

The first farmers

Farming made food supplies more reliable, so people grew stronger, lived longer and had more children. Farmers needed more land, so they cleared forests to create more fields and diverted rivers to water the crops. Some even had leisure time to built vast monuments.

This is Stonehenge, a monument built from earth and stone by early farmers using only the most basic of tools. It was begun around 5,000 years ago, and may have been used for ceremonies to celebrate important times in the farming year, such as Midwinter – when the light and warmth needed for crops began to return.

Big cities

Over time, farms grew into villages, and villages swelled into towns. By around 7,000 years ago, the first cities had arrived. They had powerful rulers who controlled the farmland around the city, and became rich and powerful by trading and selling things.

Over time, they built bigger houses with piped water and fireplaces for heating and cooking. More and more people went to live in cities, so they could have these things too.

Getting bigger

As cities kept on growing, so did the number of people in them. They needed more food, water, clothes, building materials and land to live on. More forests were cut down to make room for bigger cities and more farmland – and to provide more building wood and fire wood – changing the landscape forever.

Wild places

Even the biggest early cities only took up a fairly small amount of space. There were still vast areas of land and sea too remote for people to reach, where plants and animals thrived. But this wasn't going to last long.

Keeping a record

Farmers living near early cities often had to give part of their crop to local officials. Experts think writing may have developed to help to keep track of which farmers had delivered which crops.

Water supplies

By around 5,000 years ago, people in cities such as Mohenjo Daro in Pakistan were building water wells lined with bricks. They also had clay drain pipes to take away waste water and a big public bath for people to wash in.

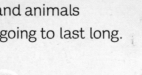

59

Age of steam

One of the biggest breakthroughs of the modern age was the invention of the coal-powered steam engine.

Steam engines drove huge ships and factory machines. They also powered trains including the Rocket, an early locomotive built in 1829 by British engineer George Stephenson.

Petroleum

Petroleum is a dark oil found in rocks. It formed when masses of tiny sea creatures fell to the ocean floor and were covered by mud. Over millions of years, more mud squashed them, until the carbon in their bodies turned into oil.

Petroleum oil

The modern world

Around 300 years ago in Europe, there was a dramatic change, known as the Industrial Revolution. It started when scientists realized that, by burning coal, they could power large engines for huge ships and trains, and big machines for vast factories.

Dirty power

Coal power brought many advantages. Factories made things more quickly and cheaply than ever before, and trains and ships took people and things around the world far faster, too. But burning coal filled the air with dirty, smelly smoke that coated everything in black soot and made it difficult for people to breathe.

Petroleum and electricity

Soon, inventors started looking for new, coal-free ways of powering machines. In the 1800s they created engines that burned fuels made from an oil called petroleum. And around 1850, electric lights and motors were invented.

Thanks to the technology of petroleum and electricity, over the next 100 years all kinds of amazing inventions came into being, including telephones, radios, X-rays, planes, cars, televisions and computers.

Modern machines

New inventions helped people to do astonishing things. Scientists discovered ways of treating diseases, saving countless lives. People on different sides of the planet could speak to each other by telephone and visit each other by plane.

Space race

In 1969, millions watched on television as astronauts landed on the moon. They brought back amazing pictures. For the first time, humans saw their planet as a small blue dot floating in space. It seemed small and fragile – and people started to realize that it is.

Sputnik

Communications satellites are machines floating in space. They are used to beam phone calls, television pictures or radio messages around the Earth. The first communications satellite, named Sputnik, was launched in 1957 from a site in Kazakhstan.

This photograph shows the landing craft that carried the first humans to the moon. You can see the moon's surface beneath and the Earth in the sky above.

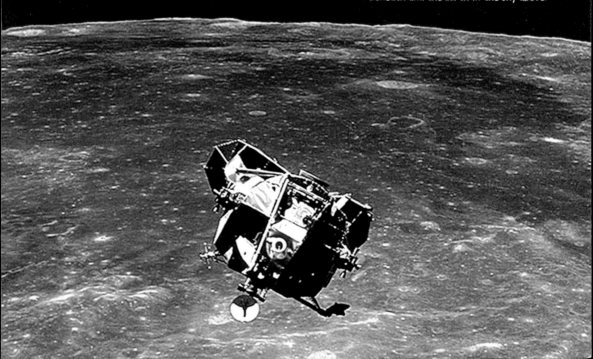

Changing planet

Recently, people have begun to realize
that even space-age technology can cause
problems for the planet, changing it in
unexpected ways. Since the end of the 20th
century, scientists have been studying these
changes, to find out what they might mean
for all of us – and for the planet –
in the future.

This picture, taken from space, shows Europe
at night. The bright dots are lights shining
out from buildings, streets and cities. They
give an idea of the huge amounts of
electricity these countries use.

People overload

In recent years, the number of people on the planet has been growing faster than ever before.

200 years ago :
1,000,000,000
people

100 years ago :
1,500,000,000
people

Today :
7,000,000,000
people

This is Chicago in the U.S.A. Big cities like this are using more and more land, power, water and food.

Planet under pressure

There are more people alive today than ever before. That means people need more food, more water, more space to grow food and build homes, more factories to make things, and more power to run all the machines, homes and cars.

Disappearing wildlife

All the land and water that people take leaves less and less for wildlife. Many factories and cities spew out pollution – harmful substances that kill plants and animals. And, now that people can travel anywhere they want, not even wild places are safe for wildlife. Many types of plants and animals are becoming extinct.

Not-so-clean power

Even more worryingly, scientists have discovered that electricity and petroleum oil aren't any cleaner than coal.

Electricity is clean once it has been made. But, to make it, people often burn coal first. And burning both coal and petroleum releases masses of CO_2 into the atmosphere.

Greenhouse gases

CO_2 is what's known as a greenhouse gas. It builds up in the Earth's atmosphere, forming a layer that traps the Sun's heat, and this warms up the planet.

It's not just people burning fossil fuels that produce CO_2 – natural things like volcanoes and lightning make it too. Some people aren't sure whether it's CO_2 from fossil fuels or from other things that's responsible for warming the planet.

Warming world

Whatever produced the CO_2 there's no doubt that it's there. Experts agree that over the last 250 years, the amount of CO_2 in the atmosphere has increased by one third. And during the last 100 years, the Earth has warmed up by around ½°C (1½°F).

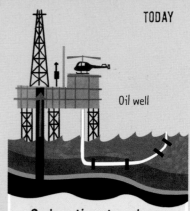

Oil well

Carbon time travel

The fossil fuels that people extract from under the ground are millions of years old. When the fuels formed, they trapped vast amounts of CO_2 from the ancient air and locked it away.

When people burn fossil fuels to make electricity, or to power cars, this unlocks the CO_2 from millions of years ago.

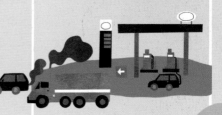

The extra CO_2 builds up in the atmosphere, where it acts as a greenhouse gas, trapping the Sun's heat and warming up the planet.

Global warming?

Even though the overall temperature of the Earth is rising, that doesn't mean it feels warmer everywhere.

The weather and oceans move hot and cold air and water around the planet. They are making some places hotter and drier than before, but other places wetter and cooler.

Storm warnings

Hurricanes are violent storms that form over the oceans. If they drift over land, they can cause serious damage. Weather scientists track hurricanes as they form, using satellites in space. They send out warnings to people who live in the path of the hurricane, so they can leave before the storm arrives.

Climate change

The rise in global temperature may seem very small, but experts agree that it's already causing changes to the climate – the overall pattern of the planet's weather. That's because it's the contrast in temperature between the land and sea that creates the weather.

Weather patterns

In some parts of the world where rain used to fall regularly, there is now less rain, or no rain at all. In other places where there used to be a few bad storms every year, there are now lots of storms, and they're very bad. Across many parts of the world there are also many more devastating floods than there used to be.

Rising water

As the planet warms, other changes are also taking place. Ice sheets that cover the coldest parts of the world are slowly melting. As they melt, water from them flows to the ocean, making sea levels rise.

Water from melted ice is cold, but climbing temperatures mean seawater is still warming up. As water gets warmer it expands, so sea levels rise even more, covering more land in water.

Changing lives

Storms, droughts and floods often mean people lose their homes or can't grow their crops. And those who live on low-lying land are driven away as the sea creeps closer to their homes. But humans can often find ways to adapt to these changes. It's much harder for plants and animals.

Struggling plants and animals

Many living things are very sensitive to tiny changes in temperature. Just a little more heat than normal can kill them. And if certain plants and animals die, then the creatures that eat them may die too.

Other creatures are very highly adapted to the places where they live, such as icy areas. If these environments disappear, the creatures die.

Leaving home

Some small islands in the Pacific Ocean are disappearing underwater because of rising sea levels. People who used to live there have already had to find somewhere else to live. People from nearby islands will probably have to leave soon, too.

Coral reefs like this one are very sensitive to climate change. Coral can die if temperatures go up slightly. And if coral dies, fish and other creatures that live on a reef die too.

Water saving

In many parts of the world there's not enough clean water to go around. This will probably get worse, because of growing numbers of people and less predictable rainfall.

Scientists are working on solutions, such as drinking straws with filters inside. These let people drink any water safely.

Working together

Lots of experts around the world are working hard to find solutions to the problems of climate change. But it isn't easy.

Alternative energy

There are some power sources that don't produce CO_2, including wind power and solar power – energy from the Sun. Unfortunately, when the wind stops blowing, or the Sun isn't shining, the power stops. But people don't stop needing to run their computers, lights and cars.

So, until someone finds a clean power source that works all the time, we will still need to get some energy from sources that release CO_2.

When the wind blows, these wind turbines turn, generating electricity. But they stop when the wind stops – whereas people need electricity around the clock.

Burying the problem

Scientists are starting to find ways of capturing CO_2 released by fossil fuels, so it doesn't escape into the atmosphere and warm the planet. They're also working on all the things that use power – appliances, engines and so on – so they work more efficiently and use less power.

Biochar

Biochar is charcoal made by burning trees in a special way that keeps in their CO_2. The biochar is buried in the soil, storing the carbon for hundreds of years.

Reduce, re-use, recycle

There are lots of small changes people can make to help save the planet, too. Less CO_2 will be released from cars, planes, factories and power stations if we all reduce the amount of power we use and the amount of stuff we buy, and if we try to re-use what we can and recycle more.

Success story

People can work together to help fix global disasters. In the 1980s, scientists noticed that a vital gas called ozone was dangerously thin in part of the atmosphere.

What about the future?

We now know that people have had a huge impact on the story of Planet Earth. What happens to that story in the future depends partly on us. But it also depends on many other things we can't control.

Unexpected events have changed our world again and again, from Ice Ages to asteroid strikes and even the start of life itself. Only one thing is certain: as long as there's a Planet Earth, it will always go on changing.

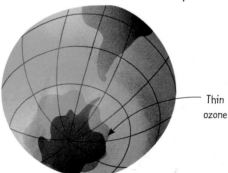

Thin ozone

The thinning was caused by gases from refrigerators, air conditioners and spray cans. Most countries have now banned the gases. The ozone is gradually repairing itself.

Timeline

This timeline shows you some of the most important things that have happened in the story of our planet. It also gives you an idea of how late in the story people arrived, compared to the hundreds of millions of years some animals have been around.

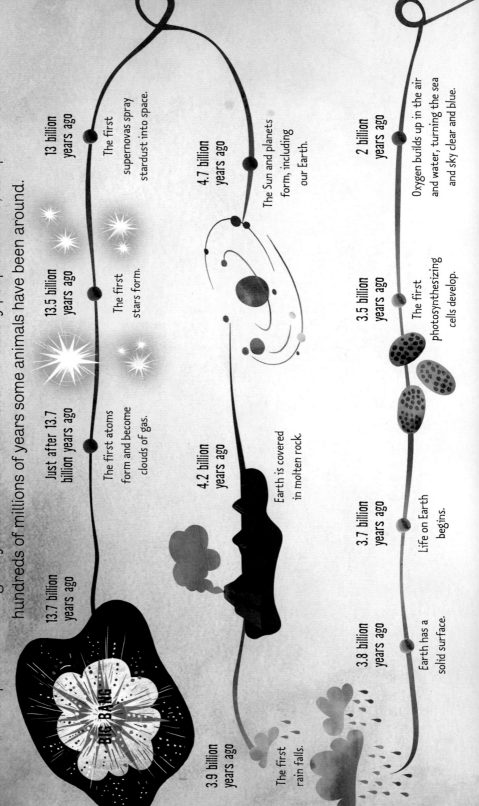

13.7 billion years ago
BIG BANG

Just after 13.7 billion years ago
The first atoms form and become clouds of gas.

13.5 billion years ago
The first stars form.

13 billion years ago
The first supernovas spray stardust into space.

4.7 billion years ago
The Sun and planets form, including our Earth.

4.2 billion years ago
Earth is covered in molten rock.

3.9 billion years ago
The first rain falls.

3.8 billion years ago
Earth has a solid surface.

3.7 billion years ago
Life on Earth begins.

3.5 billion years ago
The first photosynthesizing cells develop.

2 billion years ago
Oxygen builds up in the air and water, turning the sea and sky clear and blue.

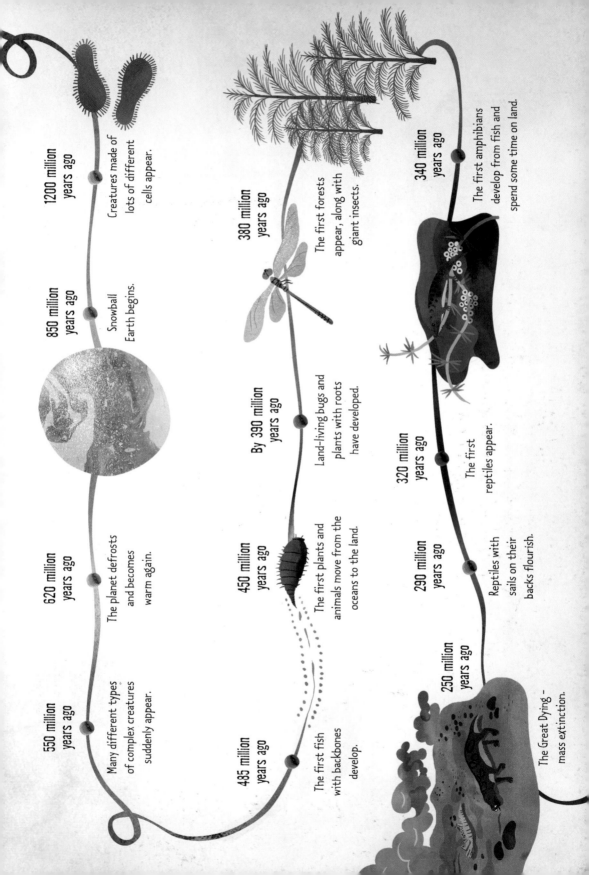

1200 million years ago

Creatures made of lots of different cells appear.

850 million years ago

Snowball Earth begins.

620 million years ago

The planet defrosts and becomes warm again.

550 million years ago

Many different types of complex creatures suddenly appear.

485 million years ago

The first fish with backbones develop.

450 million years ago

The first plants and animals move from the oceans to the land.

By 390 million years ago

Land-living bugs and plants with roots have developed.

380 million years ago

The first forests appear, along with giant insects.

340 million years ago

The first amphibians develop from fish and spend some time on land.

320 million years ago

The first reptiles appear.

290 million years ago

Reptiles with sails on their backs flourish.

250 million years ago

The Great Dying – mass extinction.

230 million years ago

The first dinosaurs appear. Some are tiny and fierce, and run around on their back legs.

By 200 million years ago

Dinosaurs have grown bigger and faster.

170 million years ago

Huge, slow, plant-eating dinosaurs have developed.

By 150 million years ago

Feathery, flying dinosaurs have appeared.

145 million years ago

Supersaurus, one of the largest ever dinosaurs, is alive.

By 140 million years ago

Stegosaurs have arrived. They have rows of plates along their backs.

By 112 million years ago

Fierce, meat-eating dinosaurs have become even bigger and scarier.

80 million years ago

Plant-eaters with bird-like beaks develop.

By 67 million years ago

Horned ceratopsian dinosaurs have appeared.

65 million years ago

Mass extinction, perhaps caused by an asteroid. End of the dinosaurs.

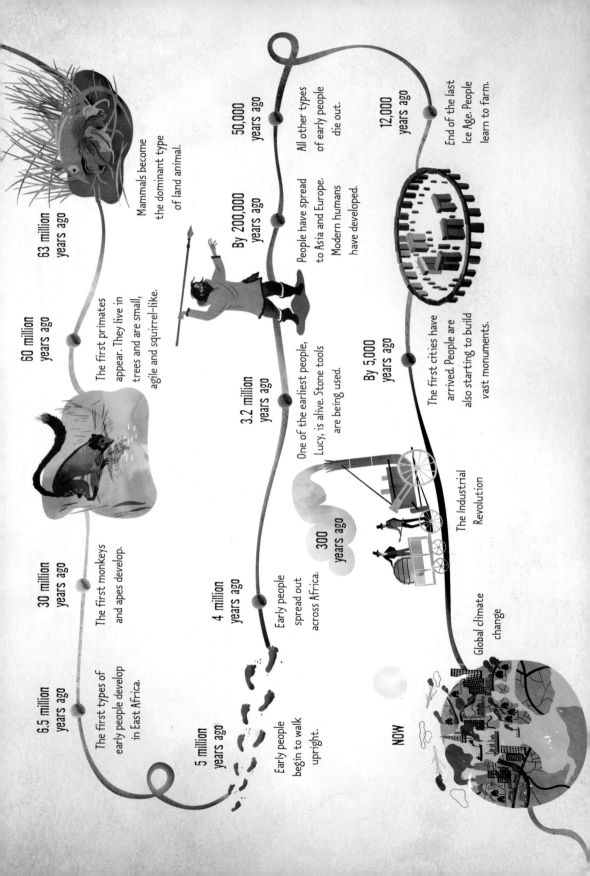

63 million
years ago

Mammals become
the dominant type
of land animal.

60 million
years ago

The first primates
appear. They live in
trees and are small,
agile and squirrel-like.

30 million
years ago

The first monkeys
and apes develop.

6.5 million
years ago

The first types of
early people develop
in East Africa.

5 million
years ago

Early people
begin to walk
upright.

4 million
years ago

Early people
spread out
across Africa.

3.2 million
years ago

One of the earliest people,
Lucy, is alive. Stone tools
are being used.

By 200,000
years ago

People have spread
to Asia and Europe.
Modern humans
have developed.

50,000
years ago

All other types
of early people
die out.

12,000
years ago

End of the last
Ice Age. People
learn to farm.

By 5,000
years ago

The first cities have
arrived. People are
also starting to build
vast monuments.

300
years ago

The Industrial
Revolution

NOW

Global climate
change

Glossary

Words that are **darker** have their own separate entries.

air A mixture of **gases**, including **oxygen** and **carbon dioxide** (CO_2), that surrounds the **Earth** and is essential for life.

amphibian A type of animal that lives partly on land and partly in water. They have moist skins and lay soft, wobbly eggs.

ankylosaur A type of **dinosaur** that was completely covered in bony plates.

asteroid A lump of rock that hurtles through **space**.

atmosphere Layers of **gases** surrounding a large object in **space**, such as the **Earth**.

atoms Extremely tiny things, formed of even tinier **particles**. Atoms can be split back into particles by **nuclear reactions**.

backbone A flexible column of bone that helps to support some animals from inside.

Big Bang The idea that the **Universe** suddenly exploded into being.

Big Whack The idea that a **planet**-sized mass known as **Theia** crashed into the early **Earth**, forming the **Moon**.

billion A thousand **million** or 1,000,000,000.

biochar A type of charcoal that captures carbon dioxide (CO_2).

CO_2 *See* **carbon dioxide**.

carbon A type of **atom** that is in many things including **carbon dioxide**, **coal**, **petroleum**, and the bodies of living things.

carbon dioxide (CO_2) A type of **gas**, partly made of **carbon**, forming part of the **Earth's atmosphere**.

cells Tiny living things. They often cluster together to make larger living things such as plants and animals.

centipede A type of creature with many legs and a hard body covering known as an **exoskeleton**.

ceratopsian A type of **dinosaur** with bony frills and horns on its head.

chemical A **substance**, especially one that's involved in **chemical reactions**.

chemical reaction What happens when two or more **chemicals** mix together.

climate change Changes in the weather measured over a long period of time.

coal A type of rock that can be burned. It's formed mainly of **carbon** and made from the squashed remains of ancient forests.

cold-blooded Unable to warm up the body from inside. **Reptiles** and **amphibians** are both cold-blooded.

collision A massive crash.

continent A vast chunk of land.

coral A type of living structure that forms under the sea from many tiny creatures living very close together.

core The central part of something.

crater A hole created by the impact of a rock or **asteroid** from space.

dinosaur A group of ancient **reptiles** that became **extinct** 65 **million** years ago – though some scientists class modern birds as living dinosaurs.

dissolve To mix something into a **liquid**.

dragonfly A type of flying **insect**.

Earth The **planet** in the **Solar System** where we live.

earthquake A sudden movement in the **Earth's** surface that shakes the ground.

electricity A type of **power**.

environment A particular type of place.

evolution The way different types of living things change, or **evolve**, over time.

evolve *See* **evolution**.

exoskeleton The hard outer covering that protects the bodies of some animals.

expand To get bigger.

extinct No longer living. When a type of creature is extinct, every single one has died out. *See also* **mass extinction**.

fossil The shape of a living thing or part of a living thing, preserved in rock.

fossil fuels **Fuels** made from fossilized plants and animals, including **coal** and **petroleum oil**.

fuel Something that can be used to make **power**.

gas A light, airy **substance**.

global warming An increase in the overall **temperature** of the **planet** and **atmosphere**.

hadrosaur A type of plant-eating **dinosaur** with lots of small teeth for chewing leaves.

human All modern people are humans, and some **extinct** types of early people are counted as humans too.

Ice Age A period during which the **Earth** became extremely cold.

insect A type of six-legged animal with a hard **exoskeleton**. Most insects can fly.

life form A living thing.

liquid A wet, flowing **substance**.

lungs Parts that many creatures have inside their bodies and use for breathing.

mammal A type of hairy, **warm-blooded** creature that feeds its babies on milk.

mammoth An **extinct** hairy, elephant-like animal.

mantle A hot layer of rock around the **Earth's core** and beneath its surface.

mass extinction A time when many types of creatures die out very quickly.

methane A type of **gas**. It can build up in the **atmosphere** and trap the **Sun's** heat, warming the **planet**.

microscopic Extremely tiny.

million A thousand thousand or 1,000,000.

millipede A creature with many legs and a hard covering known as an **exoskeleton**.

molten Melted into **liquid**.

moon The huge rocky ball that circles the **Earth** and glows in the night sky.

natural selection The chance events that, along with **evolution**, mean different types of **life forms** survive or die out over time.

nautiloid A type of squid-like sea creature with a hard shell and tentacles.

nuclear reaction A process that happens when **atoms** split, creating lots of heat.

oil A slimy, liquid **substance** that can often be burned. *See also* **petroleum**.

orbit The curved path of one thing as it travels around another thing.

ornithopod A type of plant-eating **dinosaur** that had a hard, bird-like beak.

oxygen A type of **gas** that many living things need to breathe.

ozone A type of **gas** that builds up in the **Earth's atmosphere**, keeping out some of the **Sun's** harmful rays.

Pangaea A huge mass of land that existed around 280 **million** years ago.

particle An incredibly tiny thing that is part of an **atom**.

petroleum A dark, slimy **oil** found in the **Earth's** rocks. It's made of squashed ancient sea creatures.

photosynthesis The process plants use to make food from sunlight, water and **carbon dioxide gas** (CO_2).

planet A vast ball of rock or **gas orbiting** a star such as the **Sun**.

plates Vast sections of the **Earth's** rock that move very slowly across the surface of the **planet**.

plesiosaur A type of **extinct**, sea-dwelling **reptile** with a long neck and sharp teeth.

pollution **Substances** that can harm plants and animals.

power A measure of the amount of work done, or energy used, in a particular time.

primate A group of **mammals** suited to climbing trees, including monkeys, apes and **humans**.

recycle To make used things into new things.

release To let something out.

reproduce To copy something.

reptile A type of **cold-blooded**, scaly-skinnned creature.

sauropod A type of slow, plant-eating **dinosaur** with a long neck and a big body. Many sauropods were huge.

sea level The height of the surface of the ocean compared to the land.

skeleton A hard framework, often made of bone, on the inside of the animals that helps to hold them up.

Snowball Earth The idea that the **Earth** was completely or mostly covered in ice for around 250 **million** years.

Solar System The **Sun**, the **planets**, including **Earth**, and other objects that **orbit** around the **Sun**.

space The area that surrounds all the **stars**, **planets** and other things in the **Universe**.

star A vast, burning fireball in **space**, powered by **nuclear reactions** taking place inside it.

stardust Tiny grains made up of different **atoms** sprayed out by **stars**. Star dust mixes with great clouds of **gas** in space.

steam Water that has turned to **gas**, or **droplets** of **liquid** water in the air.

stegosaur A type of **dinosaur** with rows of bony plates along its back.

substance Any particular type of stuff.

Sun The **star** around which all the **planets** in the **Solar System**, including the **Earth**, **orbit**.

telescope Something designed to help people to see things that are far away.

temperature How hot something is.

Theia A huge, **planet**-like mass that's thought to have crashed into the early **Earth**, forming the **Moon**.

theropod A type of **dinosaur** that walked on its back legs.

trilobite An **extinct** type of sea creature that scuttled along the sea bed. Trilobites had hard coverings or **exoskeletons**.

tsunamis Giant, destructive waves in the seas and oceans, often caused by **earthquakes**.

Universe A name for everything that exists and all of **space** and time.

ultraviolet A type of ray from the **Sun** that can damage the skin of people and animals.

vent An opening where heat and **chemicals** well up from under the **Earth's** surface.

volcano Openings in the **Earth's** surface where **molten** rock and **gases** spout up from underneath.

warm-blooded Able to warm up the body from inside. Birds and **mammals** are both warm-blooded.

wildlife All wild plants, animals and other living things.

wind turbine A structure with large, turning blades that converts wind **power** into **electricity**.

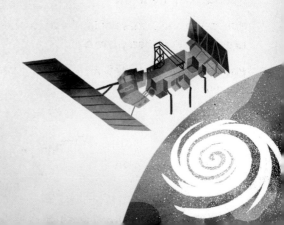

Index

Acknowledgements

Every effort has been made to trace the copyright holders of material in this book. If any rights have been omitted, the publishers offer their sincere apologies and will rectify this in any subsequent editions following notification. The publishers are grateful to the following organizations and individuals for their permission to reproduce material on the following pages: (t = top, b = bottom, l = left, r = right)

Cover: Planetary Visions Ltd / Science Photo Library
pp2-3: Tom McHugh/Science Photo Library; pp4-5: Stephen & Donna O'Meara/Science Photo Library; pp6-7: Roger Harris/Science Photo Library; p8 (t): Jose Antonio Peñas/Science Photo Library; p9 (b): Claus Lunau/ Science Photo Library; p10 (t): Kevin A Horgan/Science Photo Library; pp12-13: Detlev Van Ravenswaay/Science Photo Library; p16 (t): NASA Jet Propulsion Laboratory (NASA-JPL); p17 (b): Take 27 Ltd/Science Photo Library; pp18-19 (tr): Paul Wootton/Science Photo Library; p20 (t): Walter Myers/Science Photo Library; pp22-23: © eye35 stock / Alamy; p25 (b): © Stocktrek Images, Inc. / Alamy; p26 (t): Biophoto Associates/Science Photo Library; p27 (t): Gerd Guenther/Science Photo Library; p28 (b): Nicolas Dubreuil/Look at Sciences/Science Photo Library; p29 (t): Simon Terrey/Science Photo Library; p30 (t): © Stocktrek Images, Inc. / Alamy; p31 (b): Walter Myers/Science Photo Library; pp32-33: Christian Darkin/Science Photo Library; pp34-35: Walter Myers/Science Photo Library; p36 (t): Walter Myers/Science Photo Library; p37 (b): Walter Myers/Science Photo Library; p39 (t): Walter Myers/Science Photo Library; p40 (b): Walter Myers/Science Photo Library; pp42-43: © Corey Ford/Stocktrek Images/ Corbis; p46 (b): Roger Harris/Science Photo Library; p47 (t): Mark Garlick/Science Photo Library; p48 (t): Mark Garlick/Science Photo Library; p50 (b): Walter Myers/Science Photo Library; p51 (t): © Pete Oxford / naturepl.com; pp52-53: © Copyright 2002-2010 Nature Picture Library. All rights reserved; p54 (b): © Viktor Deak; p57 (b): Philippe Psaila/Science Photo Library; p58 (b): ajliikala/Flickr/Getty Images; p61 (b): NASA; pp62-63: Planetary Visions Ltd / Science Photo Library; p64 (b): © Jason Lindsey / Alamy; p67 (b): © Georgette Douwma/ naturepl.com; p68 (b): © Jon Boyes/Tetra Images/Corbis

Managing designer: Stephen Moncrieff
Additional design by Emily Barden, Will Dawes, Nelupa Hussein and Steve Wood
Digital designs by John Russell
Art Director: Mary Cartwright
Picture research by Ruth King

With thanks to Professor Dan Tovey